Cultivating Success

A Strategic Guide to Small Business Growth

Rachel Smith

Table of content

Introduction

Chapter 1: Strategic Planning for Growth

Chapter 2: Marketing Mastery and Branding

Chapter 3: Financial Fitness and Fiscal Responsibility

Chapter 4: Operational Excellence and Efficiency

Chapter5: Customer-Centric Approach for Lasting Success

Introduction

Welcome to "Cultivating Success: A Strategic Guide to Small Business Growth." In the shifting environment of entrepreneurship, navigating the route to sustained success takes a combination of vision, strategy, and perseverance. Drawing upon two decades of professional experience, this book serves as your trusted guide on the quest to not only survive but flourish in the world of small company.

In the following chapters, we will discuss fundamental ideas and practical insights that transcend industry borders. From building a compelling vision and defining strategic objectives to mastering the art of customer-centricity, each chapter is intended to provide you with practical tools and proven tactics. Whether you're a seasoned entrepreneur or just beginning your business adventure, "Cultivating Success" is your guide to unlocking the full potential of your small firm and creating a legacy of lasting success. Let's begin on this revolutionary trip together.

Chapter 1

Strategic Planning for Growth

Navigating the intricacies of the corporate world demands a strategy that extends beyond day-to-day operations. Strategic planning for growth is the compass that steers businesses toward their future, giving a disciplined way to capitalize on opportunities and solve problems. In the following examination, we dig into the delicate art of strategic planning, revealing the underlying concepts that support sustained development and success.

A. Crafting a Vision for Your Business

In the opening portion of "Cultivating Success," we dig into the basic cornerstone of small company growth—crafting a captivating vision. A vision acts as the North Star, leading your firm through the ever-evolving marketplace.

Unveiling the Entrepreneurial Landscape:
Embark on a tour through the entrepreneurial world, where options abound and obstacles are opportunities in disguise. This part emphasizes the dynamic nature of small enterprises, highlighting the necessity for a clear vision to manage the difficulties.

The Essence of Vision:
Define the nature of vision and its role in driving your firm toward success. We discuss how a well-crafted vision statement goes beyond simple words; it becomes the lifeblood of your organization, motivating stakeholders and uniting efforts towards a shared goal.

Visionaries in Action:
Drawing inspiration from real-world examples, this section displays exceptional entrepreneurs who converted their dreams into profitable enterprises. Their stories serve as beacons, illustrating the tangible impact a powerful vision can have on organizational culture, innovation, and sustained growth.

Navigating Challenges with Vision:
Business landscapes are riddled with uncertainty. Discover how a powerful vision functions as a compass during stormy times, helping you to make educated choices and pivot effectively. We analyze case studies of organizations that withstood crises by sticking to their basic goal.

Crafting Your Vision:
Guiding you through the process of writing a vision statement specific to your firm, this part includes practical frameworks and activities. Learn how to compress your ambitions into a brief, effective statement that connects with both internal teams and external stakeholders.

Aligning Teams with Vision:
Explore ways for building a common vision among your team members. Effective communication and alignment of individual functions with the larger goal generate a synergy that pushes the organization forward. Gain insights on leadership approaches that foster a vision-driven culture.

Setting the Stage for Success:
As we end the first portion, we reflect on how a well-crafted vision sets the framework for future success. Whether you're establishing a new endeavor or renewing an existing one, this chapter provides the basis for the strategic path ahead, allowing you to convert your vision into the driving force behind your small business's success.

B. Setting SMART Goals for Long-Term Success

As we go further into the strategic terrain of "Cultivating Success," our attention switches to the critical function of goal setting in moving small enterprises toward sustainable success. In this part, we uncover the art and science of developing SMART goals—goals that are Specific, Measurable, Achievable, Relevant, and Time-bound.

The Power of Strategic Goal Setting: Begin with recognizing the transforming effect of having clear and strategic objectives. We investigate how the lack of well-defined goals may leave firms adrift, and conversely, how deliberate goal formulation offers a blueprint for development and accomplishment.

Demystifying SMART Goals:
Delve into the SMART criteria—a framework that takes goal creation from a conceptual exercise to a precise instrument. Understand how specificity gives clarity, measurability quantifies progress, achievability assures feasibility, relevance resonates with the larger mission, and time-bound limits inspire urgency.

Aligning Goals with Vision:
Bridge the gap between your business's mission and day-to-day operations by understanding the skill of aligning objectives with your broader vision. Discover how strategic objectives become the connective

tissue, ensuring that every action contributes significantly to the accomplishment of your bigger vision.

The Role of Measurement:
Explore the critical topic of measuring in goal planning. This section reveals how creating unambiguous measurements not only aids monitoring progress but also promotes informed decision-making. Real-world examples highlight firms that flourished by creating and developing quantifiable criteria.

Navigating Challenges and Adjusting Goals:
In the ever-evolving environment of entrepreneurship, problems are inevitable. Learn how successful small companies manage unanticipated

hurdles without sacrificing their long-term aims. Discover the art of flexibility—knowing when to change objectives while keeping committed to the broader vision.

Case Studies in Goal Achievement:
Embark on a trip via case studies showing organizations that successfully implemented SMART goal-setting processes. These tales highlight how firms, regardless of size or sector, exploited this framework to overcome problems, capitalize on opportunities, and achieve sustainable success.

Empowering Your Team:
A vision underpinned by strategic objectives is a great motivator for your team. Uncover techniques to empower

and involve your workers in goal attainment. Learn the skill of cascading objectives across the business, guaranteeing congruence at every level and generating a feeling of shared purpose.

Goal Setting as a Dynamic Process:
As we complete this section, understand that goal setting is not a one-time event but a dynamic and iterative process. Understand the necessity of frequent assessment, recalibration, and celebration of achievements. Embrace the dynamic nature of your company and ambitions as you travel the route to long-term success.

In crossing the landscape of developing SMART objectives, this part gives you with the skills and insights to translate dreams into concrete results. Whether you're a nascent startup or an established small firm, the ideas outlined here create the framework for a journey distinguished by purpose, development, and sustainable success.

Chapter 2

Marketing Mastery and Branding

In this dynamic landscape, precision in marketing and the cultivation of a compelling brand identity are not just strategies but imperatives for success. Join us on a journey where strategic insights, creative finesse, and a profound understanding of consumer psychology converge to unlock the true potential of your brand. In this exploration, we delve into the intricacies of crafting resonant messages, building lasting connections, and mastering the nuances that transform businesses into distinctive and enduring brands.

A. Building a Strong Brand Identity

In the vast marketplace of commerce, a brand is more than a name or a logo; it is the living essence of your enterprise, a narrative that resonates with your audience. Drawing upon my extensive two-decade journey in the realm of business, this exploration of 'Building a Strong Brand Identity' is not a mere guide; it is a voyage into the intricate art and science of cultivating a brand that transcends the transactional and becomes an integral part of the consumer's life.

The Foundation of Identity: Core Values and Vision

A robust brand identity begins with a profound understanding of the core values that define your business. These values are not merely statements on a wall but the guiding principles that permeate every facet of your operations. Through years of navigating diverse industries, I've witnessed brands thrive when they authentically align their actions with their declared values. We embark on a journey to excavate the fundamental beliefs that underpin your enterprise, laying the groundwork for a brand that stands not just for products but for a set of principles that resonate with your audience.

Vision, the compass that steers the ship of your enterprise, is equally pivotal. A clear and compelling vision statement serves as a North Star, guiding internal decisions and external perceptions. We explore the delicate balance between aspirational and attainable, ensuring your vision inspires both your team and your customers. Through case studies of renowned brands, we distill the essence of crafting a vision that transcends market dynamics, fostering resilience and adaptability.

The Art of Visual Expression: Logos, Colors, and Design

Visual elements form the first impression of your brand, a silent ambassador that speaks volumes.

Delving into my extensive experience, we dissect the psychology of color, the geometry of logos, and the principles of design that leave an indelible mark on the minds of consumers. From the iconic swoosh to the golden arches, we unravel the stories behind timeless logos, unveiling the alchemy that transforms symbols into beacons of recognition.

The choice of colors goes beyond aesthetics; it taps into the subconscious, evoking emotions and associations. We explore the color wheel not just as a palette but as a strategic tool, understanding how hues can convey trust, excitement, or sophistication. Design is not just about what looks good; it's about what feels right. We delve into the principles of simplicity, consistency, and versatility, ensuring your visual identity remains cohesive across diverse platforms and mediums.

Crafting a Distinctive Voice: Messaging and Tone

Your brand speaks, and its voice should be as distinctive as its appearance. In this segment, we navigate the delicate terrain of messaging and tone, exploring how language can elevate or undermine your brand. Through real-world examples, we uncover the power of storytelling, demonstrating how narratives create emotional connections that endure. We decipher the elements of tone, from the friendly banter of social media to the formal gravity of official communications, ensuring your brand communicates with a consistent and authentic voice.

Beyond the words themselves, we delve into the art of taglines and slogans. Crafting a memorable phrase is not an exercise in cleverness but a strategic endeavor to encapsulate your brand essence in a few words. We analyze taglines that have stood the test of time, distilling the principles that make them enduring mnemonic devices in the minds of consumers.

Building Trust Through Consistency: Brand Guidelines

Consistency is the bedrock upon which trust is built. A brand that wavers in its identity sends mixed signals to its audience. We explore the creation of comprehensive brand guidelines that serve as a roadmap for internal and external stakeholders. From the specifications of logo usage to the guidelines for language and imagery, we craft a blueprint that ensures every interaction with your brand reinforces rather than dilutes its identity.

Adapting to Change: Evolution Without Compromise

A brand is not a static entity; it is a living organism that evolves with time and context. While the core values remain unwavering, the expression of those values may demand adaptation. We navigate the delicate balance of evolution, exploring case studies of brands that successfully reinvented themselves without losing their essence. In a rapidly changing marketplace, the ability to pivot without compromising authenticity is a hallmark of enduring brands.

'Building a Strong Brand Identity' is not a checklist; it is a philosophy. Through the lens of experience, we decipher the intricate dance between vision and execution, aesthetics and substance. Crafting a brand is not a one-time endeavor but a continuous commitment to authenticity, consistency, and resonance. As you embark on this journey, remember that a strong brand identity is not just a reflection of your business—it is a mirror that your customers hold up to see themselves reflected in the values they cherish.

B. Leveraging Digital Marketing Channels Effectively

In the dynamic landscape of modern business, mastering the art of digital marketing is indispensable. Drawing from two decades of hands-on experience, this discourse on 'Leveraging Digital Marketing Channels Effectively' transcends the theoretical and delves into practical insights honed through navigating the ever-evolving realm of online commerce.

Understanding the Digital Terrain

The digital environment is broad, including a multiplicity of channels, each with its own characteristics. From social networking platforms to search engines, email, and beyond, the possibilities are immense. Yet, the key lies not in ubiquitous presence but in strategic selection. It's about understanding where your audience resides and aligning your efforts accordingly. We delve into the analytics of audience behavior, unraveling the data to guide your choices and maximize your impact.

In a society overwhelmed by information, attention is a precious commodity. Crafting narratives that resonate amidst the digital cacophony is an art. Through realistic examples and real-world campaigns, we study the anatomy of captivating content. Whether via the brief charm of a tweet, the immersive force of a video, or the informational depth of a blog article, we decipher the aspects that attract, engage, and convert.

Social Media Mastery

Social media is not simply a platform; it's a community. Navigating this dynamic landscape needs precision. From the fleeting attraction of Instagram stories to the professional networking on LinkedIn, we explore the techniques that utilize each platform's distinct characteristics. Moreover, we untangle the algorithmic riddle, knowing how to naturally boost your reach and intelligently spend in paid advertising for best outcomes.

Optimizing for Search Engines

In the broad expanse of the internet, visibility is crucial. Understanding the algorithms that drive search engines is equivalent to opening digital doors to your company. We go into the science of SEO (Search Engine Optimization), demystifying the subtleties of keywords, backlinks, and user experience. Effective SEO is not a one-time fix but a constant process of refining, and we build a path for ongoing exposure.

Email Marketing Excellence

Email, frequently underrated, is a formidable weapon when used with accuracy. From creating subscriber lists to producing newsletters that convert, we examine the subtleties of successful email marketing. Personalization, segmentation, and automation are not simple buzzwords but strategic imperatives that boost engagement and cultivate enduring consumer connections.

Data-Driven Decision Making

In the digital environment, data is the compass that leads your trip. We explore the numbers that matter, from click-through rates to conversion funnels. However, data is not just about statistics; it's about insights. Through case studies and practical implementations, we understand the tales data tells, helping you to make educated choices and change your tactics in real-time.

Adapting to Trends Without Losing Core Identity

Digital marketing is a region of perpetual innovation. What works now may not tomorrow. Yet, the key is not mindless adaptation but strategic development. We analyze case studies of companies that adeptly accepted evolving trends without compromising their essential character. From viral challenges to influencer partnerships, we analyze the intricacies of trend adoption with authenticity.

Leveraging Digital Marketing Channels Effectively is not a handbook but a compass. It's a guide forged through years of navigating the digital frontier. As you travel the internet terrain, remember that the core of good digital marketing resides not only in exposure but in real interactions. It's about being where your consumer is, speaking a language they understand, and giving value that exceeds the transactional. In the digital arena, success is not just about clicks; it's about building a lasting imprint in the minds and hearts of your digital audience.

Chapter 3

Financial Fitness and Fiscal Responsibility

In the complex landscape of personal and corporate finance, achieving financial fitness and embracing fiscal responsibility are pivotal to long-term success. With two decades of experience navigating the intricate nuances of financial matters, I've witnessed the transformative impact of sound financial practices on individuals and businesses alike. In this exploration, we delve into the core principles that underpin financial fitness, offering insights and strategies that stand the test of time. Join me on this journey toward fiscal well-being, where prudent financial decisions pave the way for enduring prosperity and resilience.

A. Budgeting for Growth and Stability

In the intricate tapestry of business management, few elements are as crucial as the art and science of budgeting. Drawing upon two decades of navigating the ever-shifting terrain of commerce, this exploration of 'Budgeting for Growth and Stability' is not a theoretical discourse but a pragmatic guide forged through the crucible of real-world challenges and triumphs.

At the heart of financial prowess lies a well-crafted budget. It's not merely a spreadsheet of numbers but a roadmap that aligns aspirations with fiscal realities. Through the lens of experience, we delve into the foundational principles of budgeting, dissecting the intricate dance between revenue projections, cost allocations, and profit margins. A robust budget is not a rigid constraint but a dynamic instrument that flexes with the pulse of your business. We explore the elements that constitute a comprehensive budget, from fixed costs to variable expenses, leaving no stone unturned in the pursuit of financial foresight.

Aligning Budgets with Strategic Objectives

A budget devoid of strategic alignment is a compass without direction. We explore the symbiotic relationship between budgeting and strategic planning. Your financial plan should mirror your business objectives, whether it be expansion into new markets, product diversification, or streamlining operations for efficiency. Through case studies and practical insights, we unravel the strategies employed by successful enterprises to integrate financial planning seamlessly with their overarching business goals. In essence, a budget is not a constraint but a catalyst for growth when aligned with a strategic vision.

Investing in Innovation and Future Growth

In a landscape where innovation is the currency of progress, budgeting serves as the financial launchpad for transformative initiatives. We navigate the delicate balance of allocating resources for immediate needs while earmarking funds for innovation and future growth. From research and development to technology adoption, we explore how visionary budgeting propels businesses beyond the confines of the present, fostering resilience and relevance in an ever-evolving market.

Risk Mitigation and Contingency Planning

The business terrain is fraught with uncertainties, and prudent budgeting is a shield against the unforeseen. Through the lens of experience, we dissect the art of risk assessment and contingency planning. A robust budget anticipates potential pitfalls and allocates resources to create financial buffers. We explore the methodologies employed by seasoned professionals to identify, assess, and mitigate risks, ensuring that your financial plan is not just a blueprint for success but a resilient fortress against adversity.

B. Cash Flow Management: The Lifeline of Stability

Cash flow is the lifeblood of any enterprise. It's not just about revenue and expenses on paper but the liquidity that sustains day-to-day operations. We delve into the intricacies of effective cash flow management, exploring the delicate balance between receivables and payables. Through practical examples, we uncover the strategies to optimize working capital, ensuring that your business not only survives but thrives in both prosperous and challenging times.

Performance Metrics: Beyond the Balance Sheet

Financial health extends beyond the balance sheet. We navigate the realm of performance metrics, exploring key indicators that provide a comprehensive view of your business's fiscal vitality. From profitability ratios to return on investment, we decipher the language of financial metrics, empowering you to gauge the effectiveness of your budgeting strategies and pivot when necessary.

Through practical applications, we unveil the insights these metrics offer, transforming them from numbers on a page to actionable intelligence.

Building a Culture of Fiscal Responsibility

Budgeting is not a solitary endeavor confined to the finance department; it's a collaborative effort that permeates the organizational culture. We explore how to instill a culture of fiscal responsibility, where every team member understands the impact of their decisions on the financial health of the company. Through communication strategies and training initiatives, we unravel the methods employed by successful business leaders to foster a collective commitment to fiscal prudence.

Scaling Operations: Budgeting for Efficiency

As businesses evolve, so do their operational needs. Scaling efficiently requires astute budgeting that anticipates the demands of growth without succumbing to bloat. We explore the intricacies of scaling operations without compromising financial stability. From workforce expansion to infrastructure investments, we chart a course that ensures growth is not just a numerical increase but a strategic elevation of your business's capabilities.

Navigating Economic Shifts: Adapting Budgets to External Dynamics

The external landscape, with its economic shifts and market dynamics, is beyond our control. However, a seasoned business leader doesn't react; they respond. We delve into the strategies employed by professionals to adapt budgets to external dynamics, whether it be economic downturns, regulatory changes, or shifts in consumer behavior. A resilient budget is not a rigid script but an adaptable playbook that responds to the ever-changing cadence of the business environment.

Stakeholder Communication: Transparency and Accountability

it's a communication tool the art of transparent communication, ensuring that investors, employees, and other stakeholders understand the financial narrative of your business. Transparency builds trust, and trust is the currency that sustains long-term partnerships. Through practical insights, we unravel the strategies to communicate financial performance with clarity and accountability.

In essence, 'Budgeting for Growth and Stability' is not a theoretical treatise but a field guide. It's a compendium of insights and strategies distilled through the crucible of practical experience. As you embark on the journey of financial planning, remember that a budget is not a constraint; it's a strategic tool that empowers your business to not only weather storms but navigate towards new horizons of growth and stability.

Effective Cash Flow Management: Navigating the Financial Currents

In the delicate dance of firm finance, efficient cash flow management emerges as a key for sustained success. Drawing upon two decades of hands-on experience in the labyrinth of commerce, this exploration of 'Effective Cash Flow Management' is not a theoretical dissertation but a pragmatic guide, etched with the lessons learned from tides of financial ebb and flow.

The Essence of Cash Flow: Beyond Profit and Loss

Cash flow is the lifeblood of every firm, a throbbing rhythm that underpins daily operations. It's not confined to profit and loss statements but encapsulates the liquidity that fuels business vitality. Through the lens of seasoned experience, we dissect the essence of cash flow, demystifying its components from accounts receivable and payable to operational expenses. A deep dive into the intricacies reveals that profitability on paper is meaningless if it doesn't translate into actual cash in hand.

Anticipating the Peaks and Valleys: Prudent Forecasting

In the realm of cash flow, foresight is a superpower. We explore the art of prudent forecasting, where historical data, market trends, and operational realities converge to project the financial landscape ahead. Through case studies and practical insights, we unravel the strategies employed by seasoned professionals to anticipate the peaks and valleys, ensuring that your business sails through turbulence with financial resilience.

Working Capital Optimization: Balancing the Equation

Working capital is the lifeblood that lubricates the operational machinery.

We delve into the delicate equilibrium of optimizing working capital, understanding that excessive liquidity can be as detrimental as a shortage. From inventory management to efficient receivables and payables cycles, we chart a course that ensures your business operates with the ideal blend of agility and stability. Through real examples, we unravel the techniques to achieve this delicate balance, boosting operational efficiency without tying up surplus resources.

Strategic Receivables Management: Turning Sales into Cash

A sale is not complete until the cash is in hand. We explore the nuances of strategic receivables management, unraveling the techniques to accelerate cash collection without jeopardizing client relationships. From credit terms negotiation to invoice factoring, we chart a roadmap that transforms sales into tangible liquidity, fostering a healthy cash flow cycle.

Tackling Overhead Costs: Pruning for Efficiency

Overhead costs, if left unchecked, can become silent leeches on your cash reserves. We navigate the landscape of operational expenses, exploring the strategies to prune overhead costs without compromising productivity. From technology investments that enhance efficiency to renegotiating vendor contracts, we unravel the methods employed by seasoned professionals to ensure that every expenditure aligns with tangible returns.

Leveraging Technology for Efficiency: Cash Flow Management Tools

In the digital age, technology is not just a convenience but a strategic asset. We explore the arsenal of cash flow management tools that empower businesses to navigate financial currents with precision. From cloud-based accounting platforms to predictive analytics, we delve into the technologies that transform cash flow management from a reactive task to a proactive strategy. Through practical insights, we unveil the power of real-time data in making informed decisions that steer your business towards financial stability.

Contingency Planning: Safeguarding Against Financial Storms

In the unpredictable seas of business, storms are inevitable. Effective cash flow management is not only about normal navigation; it's about planning for tempests. We explore the art of contingency planning, deciphering how seasoned professionals create financial buffers to weather economic downturns, sudden market shifts, or unexpected disruptions. Through case studies, we examine the tactics that convert unanticipated problems into opportunities for resilience and development.

Investment Decisions: Balancing Expansion and Liquidity

Business growth often demands investment, but strategic cash flow management is about balancing expansion aspirations with the imperative of liquidity. We navigate the decision-making process, exploring how to fund expansion initiatives without compromising the financial stability of your core operations. From capital budgeting to evaluating ROI, we unravel the methodologies employed by successful business leaders to ensure that growth initiatives are not just visionary but financially sustainable.

Building a Culture of Financial Responsibility: Every Team Member Counts

Effective cash flow management is not just a task for the finance department; it's a collective responsibility. We investigate ways to develop a culture of financial knowledge and accountability across all levels of the company. From staff training on cost-conscious procedures to honest communication about financial objectives, we expose the techniques to guarantee that every team member knows their part in the financial success of the organization.

Continuous Monitoring and Adaptation: The Rhythm of Financial Resilience

Cash flow management is not a one-time effort but a continuing rhythm. We delve into the strategies of continuous monitoring, where financial data is not just collected but analyzed for actionable insights. From regular cash flow statements to scenario planning, we unravel the methods employed by seasoned professionals to adapt their strategies in real-time, ensuring that your business remains agile and resilient in the face of evolving financial landscapes.

Effective Cash Flow Management is not a theoretical manifesto but a captain's log, recording the methods created over years of navigating financial currents. As you begin on the road of cash flow management, remember that it's not just about the numbers on paper; it's about orchestrating a symphony that harmonizes liquidity with growth, ensuring that your firm not only survives but flourishes in the undulating seas of economic dynamics.

Chapter 4

Welcome to the land of Operational Excellence and Efficiency, where accuracy meets productivity, and smooth processes define success. In the evolving environment of business, a seasoned awareness of operational subtleties is not simply a need; it's the cornerstone upon which strong organizations are constructed. Embarking on a journey through the lens of a 20-year veteran in the realm of business, let's delve into the strategies, methodologies, and nuances that propel organizations toward unparalleled operational mastery. Get ready to explore the art and science of optimizing processes, maximizing efficiency, and charting a course toward excellence in every facet of operations.

A.Streamlining Processes for Productivity: A Symphony of Operational Excellence

In the intricate tapestry of business management, the quest for optimal productivity is a perennial symphony. Drawing upon two decades of navigating the operational intricacies of diverse industries, this exploration of 'Streamlining Processes for Productivity' transcends the theoretical, offering practical insights etched with the nuances of hands-on experience.

The Imperative of Streamlining: Beyond Efficiency to Excellence

In a world where time is a precious commodity, the ability to streamline processes emerges as a strategic imperative. It's not merely about efficiency but the orchestration of operations into a harmonious symphony of excellence. Through the lens of seasoned experience, we delve into the essence of streamlining, deciphering the methods to enhance productivity without sacrificing quality. It's a journey beyond cost-cutting; it's a relentless pursuit of operational mastery.

Understanding the Anatomy of Processes: From Chaos to Clarity

Processes are the arteries that pulse life into organizational functions. We explore the anatomy of processes, dissecting the labyrinth of workflows to identify bottlenecks, redundancies, and inefficiencies. Through case studies and practical insights, we unravel the strategies employed by seasoned professionals to transform operational chaos into streamlined clarity. It's not just about mapping processes but understanding their symbiotic relationships and optimizing them for collective efficiency.

Technology as a Catalyst: Tools for Process Optimization

In the digital age, technology is not a mere convenience but a catalyst for process optimization. We explore the arsenal of technological tools that empower businesses to streamline operations seamlessly. From workflow automation to data analytics, we look into the technologies that convert manual procedures into agile, data-driven workflows. Through practical applications, we expose the potential of technology in improving productivity and establishing a culture of continuous improvement.

Human-Centric Design: Aligning Processes with Human Potential

Processes are not mechanical gears; they are pathways shaped by human interactions. We navigate the terrain of human-centric process design, understanding that the most efficient processes resonate with the capabilities and potential of the people executing them. From employee feedback mechanisms to collaborative design thinking, we unravel the methodologies employed by seasoned professionals to align processes with the inherent strengths and aspirations of their teams.

Eliminating Redundancies: Precision in Every Action

Redundancies are the silent thieves of productivity. We explore the strategies to identify and eliminate redundant tasks, ensuring that every action contributes meaningfully to the overarching goals of the organization. From lean procedures to Kaizen principles, we explore the ways utilized by successful organizations to build a culture of continuous improvement, where duplication is not tolerated but turned into chances for refinement.

Cross-Functional Collaboration: Breaking Silos for Synergy

In the current company environment, silos are impediments that hamper productivity. We dig into the art of cross-functional cooperation, revealing the ways to break down departmental walls and build synergy. From collaborative platforms to interdepartmental training programs, we investigate the approaches adopted by seasoned professionals to establish an organizational culture where the collective intellect of various teams fosters creativity and productivity.

Agile Methodologies: Flexibility in the Face of Change

The corporate environment is changing, and procedures must react with agility. We explore the principles of agile methodologies, understanding that flexibility is not a compromise but a strength. Through case studies, we unravel the strategies employed by businesses to embrace change, iterate rapidly, and maintain operational excellence even in the face of unforeseen challenges. Agile processes are not just responsive; they are resilient pillars of productivity.

Data-Driven Decision Making: Insights for Operational Mastery

Data is the compass that guides operational decisions. We navigate the landscape of data-driven decision-making, understanding that insights derived from data are not just metrics but strategic intelligence. From operational analytics to performance metrics, we unravel the methodologies employed by seasoned professionals to make informed decisions that elevate processes from mere tasks to strategic instruments of productivity.

Employee Training and Development: Nurturing Operational Expertise

Operational excellence is not a solitary endeavor but a collective pursuit. We explore the strategies of employee training and development, understanding that a skilled workforce is the backbone of streamlined processes. From continuous training programs to mentorship initiatives, we delve into the methodologies employed by seasoned professionals to nurture operational expertise within their teams, creating a workforce that not only executes tasks but excels in operational mastery.

Quality Assurance: Ensuring Excellence in Every Output

Streamlining processes does not mean compromising on quality. We navigate the realm of quality assurance, unraveling the strategies to embed excellence into every step of the operational workflow. From quality control measures to continuous feedback loops, we explore the methodologies employed by successful businesses to ensure that streamlining processes goes hand-in-hand with delivering outputs that exceed expectations.

Lean Thinking: Maximizing Value, Minimizing Waste

In the pursuit of streamlined processes, lean thinking emerges as a guiding principle. We explore the essence of maximizing value while minimizing waste, understanding that every step in a process should contribute meaningfully to the end goal. Through case studies and practical applications, we unravel the strategies employed by businesses to infuse lean thinking into their operational DNA, fostering a culture where efficiency is not just a goal but a mindset.

Environmental Sustainability: Processes Aligned with Responsibility

In an age of heightened environmental concern, simplifying operations goes beyond efficiency to responsibility. We study the techniques to link operational processes with sustainability objectives, realizing that environmentally sensitive actions are not merely ethical but contribute to long-term company resilience. From supply chain optimizations to waste reduction initiatives, we unravel the methodologies employed by businesses to integrate environmental sustainability into their streamlined operations.

In essence, 'Streamlining Processes for Productivity' is not a theoretical thesis but a playbook. It's a compendium of insights and strategies distilled through the crucible of practical experience. As you embark on the journey of operational excellence, remember that it's not just about efficiency gains; it's about orchestrating a symphony where every process, like a musical note, contributes to the harmonious success of the entire organization.

B. Implementing Scalable Operational Models: A Strategic Approach

In the ever-evolving landscape of contemporary business, the implementation of scalable operational models stands as a critical determinant of sustained success and resilience. With over two decades of expertise in business writing, I've observed the nuanced strategies that distinguish thriving organizations in their pursuit of operational excellence.

Understanding Scalability:

Scalability is the cornerstone of operational resilience, representing the art of orchestrating growth seamlessly while preserving performance and cost-effectiveness. This multifaceted concept demands a holistic approach, intertwining technological innovation, procedural finesse, and adept workforce management.

Strategic Planning:

Embarking on the scalability journey necessitates meticulous strategic planning. Organizations must perform a detailed study of their present operations, forecast future needs, and connect operational goals with broader company objectives. A robust strategic blueprint becomes the guiding beacon, steering decision-making processes across the organizational spectrum.

Technological Integration:

At the core of any scalable operating model lies the seamless integration of cutting-edge technology. Cloud computing, automation, and data analytics play pivotal roles in streamlining processes, enhancing efficiency, and providing the agility required to accommodate the inevitable ebbs and flows of growth.

Agile Processes:

The adoption of agile methodologies emerges as a pivotal factor in maintaining operational agility. Embracing iterative development, perpetuating continuous feedback loops, and possessing the dexterity to pivot rapidly in response to market dynamics are essential facets. Agile procedures foster a culture of flexibility, helping firms to react proactively to the ever-changing tides of the business world.

Optimizing Human Capital:

Beyond technological prowess, a scalable operational model hinges on a skilled and adaptable workforce. Investments in employee training, the cultivation of a culture of continuous improvement, and the strategic attraction of top-tier talent become critical elements in constructing a resilient and scalable organizational framework.

Risk Management:

The pursuit of scalability is not devoid of inherent risks. Effective risk management becomes paramount, encompassing the anticipation of potential challenges, fortification through robust security measures, and the establishment of contingency plans. A proactive approach to risk ensures that scalability is achieved without compromising the integrity of day-to-day operations.

Measuring Success:

Implementing scalable operational models necessitates the formulation of key performance indicators (KPIs) to assess success. Regular analysis of these measures gives essential insights into the performance of the adopted techniques, permitting continual optimization and refinement.

In summary, the odyssey toward implementing scalable operational models necessitates a multifaceted approach. This involves the seamless integration of technology, strategic acumen, agile processes, human capital development, and vigilant risk management. Organizations that embrace scalability as a basic pillar of their operational strategy position themselves not only to survive but to flourish in the dynamic currents of the modern business world.

Chapter 5

Welcome to the dynamic environment of contemporary business, where the pulse of success resonates not only in transactions but in the lasting connections built via a customer-centric strategy. With two decades of navigating the various domains of corporate communication, I welcome you on a trip into the transforming potential of putting the customer at the centerpiece of strategy. In this examination, we'll unravel the threads of a customer-centric mentality, crafting a tale of durable success where firms not only meet expectations but surpass them, generating loyalty that withstands the tests of time and competition.

A. Understanding and Connecting with Your Customer Base: A Comprehensive Guide

In the rich fabric of commercial success, the skill of knowing and interacting with your consumer base emerges as a keystone. With two decades of experience in the realm of business writing, I've witnessed the evolution of strategies that distinguish thriving organizations in their quest for customer-centricity.

Understanding Your Customer Base:

At the heart of any successful business lies a deep comprehension of its customer base. This involves delving into demographics, psychographics, and behavioral patterns. Conducting thorough market research and leveraging data analytics provide the insights needed to tailor products and services to meet the specific needs and preferences of your target audience.

Building Customer Personas:

Crafting detailed customer personas is instrumental in personalizing your approach. By creating fictional characters that represent different segments of your audience, you can humanize your customers and develop a more empathetic understanding of their goals, challenges, and decision-making processes.

Utilizing Customer Feedback:

The voice of the customer is a powerful tool. Actively seeking and valuing customer feedback, whether through surveys, reviews, or direct interactions, provides invaluable insights. Analyzing this feedback not only identifies areas for improvement but also fosters a sense of transparency and responsiveness that strengthens the customer-business relationship.

Data-Driven Decision Making:

Harnessing the power of data is paramount in the quest to understand your customer base. Utilizing customer relationship management (CRM) systems and advanced analytics enables businesses to track customer interactions, identify patterns, and make informed decisions that align with customer expectations.

Personalization and Customization:

Customers crave personalized experiences. Tailoring your products, services, and communications based on individual preferences enhances the overall customer experience. This could range from personalized recommendations to targeted marketing campaigns that resonate with specific segments of your audience.

Effective Communication Strategies:

Connecting with your consumer base takes smart communication. Crafting compelling and consistent messaging across various channels ensures that your brand resonates with your audience. This involves not only conveying the features of your products but also communicating the values and ethos that your brand represents.

Embracing Omnichannel Experiences:

In the digital age, customers interact with brands through multiple channels. Ensuring a seamless experience across these channels—whether it's in-store, online, or on social media—fosters a cohesive brand image. An omnichannel approach allows customers to transition effortlessly between different touchpoints, enhancing overall satisfaction.

Adapting to Changing Customer Expectations:

Customer expectations evolve, influenced by technological advancements and shifting cultural trends. Staying alert to these changes and adjusting your strategy appropriately indicates a dedication to fulfilling the dynamic demands of your consumer base.

Community Engagement and Social Responsibility:

Modern consumers are not just transactional; they seek brands that align with their values. Engaging with communities and demonstrating social responsibility not only contributes to a positive brand image but also establishes an emotional connection with your customer base.

Measuring Customer Satisfaction:

Regularly assessing customer happiness using measures like Net Promoter Score (NPS) or customer satisfaction surveys gives quantitative information. Tracking these measures over time helps firms to assess the performance of their strategy and find areas for improvement.

The Role of Employee Engagement:

Happy and engaged staff contribute greatly to excellent customer encounters. Employees who understand and align with the values of the company can effectively convey these values to customers, creating a harmonious connection between the brand and its audience.

Understanding and connecting with your customer base is an intricate yet essential endeavor. It takes a comprehensive strategy that blends data-driven insights, tailored experiences, effective communication, and a commitment to adaptation. Organizations that focus the client experience not only generate loyalty but also position themselves as leaders in a competitive market.

B. Building Loyalty Through Exceptional Customer Experiences

In the dynamic realm of business, where competition is fierce and consumer choices abound, building lasting loyalty hinges on the creation of exceptional customer experiences. Drawing upon two decades of professional business writing, I've experienced the transforming impact of customer-centric tactics that raise businesses from transactions to lasting relationships.

Understanding   Customer Expectations:

The foundation of exceptional customer experiences lies in a deep understanding of customer expectations. This includes going beyond product features to comprehend the emotional and practical demands driving client behavior. By recognizing and anticipating these expectations, businesses can tailor their approach to resonate with the unique desires of their clientele.

Seamless Omnichannel Experiences:

In an interconnected world, customers expect a seamless experience across various touchpoints. Whether engaging through websites, mobile apps, social media, or in-store interactions, a consistent and integrated experience reinforces the brand identity. Aligning messages and services across these channels fosters a cohesive and memorable customer journey.

Personalization and Tailoring:

Customers enjoy individualized encounters that reflect their uniqueness. Leveraging data to understand client preferences allows for targeted suggestions, individualized communication, and a feeling of exclusivity. This personal touch not only meets immediate needs but also establishes a connection that extends beyond transactional encounters.

Proactive Problem Resolution:

Exceptional experiences arise not just from flawless transactions but from how challenges are handled. Proactive and efficient problem resolution demonstrates commitment to customer satisfaction. Swift responses to issues, transparent communication, and a genuine desire to resolve problems build trust and can turn a negative experience into a positive one.

Empowering Customer Engagement:

Encouraging customer engagement goes beyond transactions; it involves creating a community around the brand. This can be achieved through interactive content, loyalty programs, and social media engagement. By fostering a sense of belonging and shared values, businesses elevate customer relationships from mere transactions to ongoing partnerships.

Consistent and Transparent Communication:

Clear and consistent communication is the backbone of exceptional customer experiences. From marketing messages to post-purchase follow-ups, maintaining transparency builds trust. Honest communication about product features, pricing, and policies establishes credibility and reinforces the brand's commitment to integrity.

Employee Training and Alignment:

Frontline employees are ambassadors of the brand. Investing in employee training to enhance customer service skills and align with the brand's values is crucial. Engaged and well-trained employees create a positive atmosphere that resonates with customers, fostering a sense of confidence and satisfaction.

Surprise and Delight:

Occasionally exceeding expectations with unexpected gestures can leave a lasting impression. Whether it's a personalized thank-you note, a surprise discount, or exclusive access to new products, these gestures demonstrate a commitment to going above and beyond, creating memorable moments that customers are likely to share and cherish.

Data Security and Privacy:

In a period of heightened worries about data security, preserving client privacy is crucial. Implementing rigorous security measures and open privacy rules instills trust in consumers, informing them that their information is handled properly. This trust is a key ingredient in creating long-term loyalty.

Continuous Improvement and Adaptability:

The corporate world is changing, and consumer expectations develop. A dedication to constant development and adaptation is crucial. Regularly soliciting consumer input, remaining alert to industry trends, and being prepared to pivot based on changing demands indicate a drive to staying current and responsive.

Measuring and Analyzing Loyalty Metrics:

Implementing measures to monitor consumer loyalty is vital for improving strategy. Metrics like as Net Promoter Score (NPS), customer retention rates, and customer lifetime value give measurable insights into the success of loyalty-building programs. Regular study of these indicators directs continuous improvements.

In conclusion, developing loyalty via excellent customer experiences is an ongoing process that needs a deep knowledge of client expectations, tailored interactions, and a commitment to continual improvement. Businesses that emphasize these factors not only develop client loyalty but also position themselves as leaders in an ever-evolving industry.